LIST OF CONTENTS

Introduction

There are now so many individuals involved in the care of old people that the Scottish Health Education Unit considered that there was a need for a practical manual of guidance on general "do's" and "don'ts".

The whole field of care for the elderly has been clouded by old-fashioned notions and myths and too often has been seen exclusively as the rest of society doing things for old people who were then expected to keep quiet, behave themselves and be grateful. Caring means much more than this – providing the opportunity for old people to be as independent as possible, to continue active and positive roles and, above all, to enjoy some degree of choice in how their lives will be lived. It is essential to put the era of "custodial care" in the history book where it belongs and this manual is meant to help in this process.

The manual is intended primarily for the caring staff in old peoples' homes and institutions and for wardens in sheltered housing and it has been written by contributors from a wide range of backgrounds. Each writer has first hand experience and the information is of a practical nature.

It is hoped that many others will find the booklet useful – including members of families who are involved with their own folk and even some old people themselves will find useful hints and advice. Further editions of this publication will be produced if it is well received and it would be welcomed if interested persons who have suggestions for improving its content or presentation were to send them to the Scottish Health Education Unit, 21 Lansdowne Crescent, Edinburgh EH12 5EH
Telephone 031-337 3251

Professor J. Williamson
(City Hospital, Edinburgh)

Active Roles

Activity is the password to health. Many people find themselves busier in retirement than before and one of the pleasurable sides of this is that you can, at long last, choose what activities to follow. People of every age have a basic need to be wanted, be useful, and have a purpose in life. With time and experience available what better way of life to lead than use them to the full.

The housebound or even those confined to bed may be able to carry out a service via a telephone, writing letters or craft work. What can be done is very much an individual matter and dependent on circumstances. After 65 + years no one will change their personality to fit some role devised by others.

The following ideas are only some of the activities that may be enjoyed by the retired section of the community. Previously, much good work used to be done by the middle-aged group of women after their family commitment no longer took up a full day. Now, as more women return to full-time, paid employment this gap may be filled by active pensioners: —

1   Making 'Aids for the Elderly' — or organising the making.

2   Crafts teaching, using or learning.

3   Chiropody — providing a first aid service, using pre-retirement skills.

4   Clothes swap — through luncheon clubs etc.

5   Car service — simple maintenance, cleaning, outings, hospital service.

6   Collecting prescriptions — chronic cases.

7   Conversation practice — French, German etc, help for tourists.

Active Roles

8   Cake bakes. Individuals and groups.

9   Baby/Granny sitting services — short/long term.

10   Bulk buying via groups to cut cost of living.

11   Barber — especially for the house-bound.

12   Evening classes — participation or running.

13   Financial advice to groups and individuals.

14   Flower cultivation — arrangement, supply.

15   Friendship — lunch, theatre, cinema, bingo.

16   Football — talks, refereeing, training for schools or youth organisations.

17   Good neighbour scheme (may be paid) — filling hot water bottle, shopping, taking letters.

18   Exercising dogs, children.

19   Home library service through WRVS.

20   Health talks.

21   Garden exchange — high-rise flat dwellers to look after pensioner's patch, neighbours.

22   Hairdressing service — share equipment, domicillary service.

23   Help for housebound and disabled — with insulation, draft exclusion, over form filling, with letter writing.

24   Hospital visiting.

25   Holidays — share car, arrangements, company, hire of house, exchange house.

26   Keep Fit Class — organise or join in one.

27   Knitted squares for blankets, dish cloths, baby clothes, shawls.

28   Make jams and jellies; toys — rag dolls, wooden toys.

29   Newspapers — share cost, read to those with impaired vision.

Active Roles

30   Other sports — whatever the interest keep up connection, make scrap book.

31   Part time/paid/voluntary employment.

32   Painting — for your own enjoyment, portraits from photos.

33   Photography — at social events, help youngsters.

34   Poetry collections for and by others, own self.

35   Pets — keep own, help schools over holiday periods, keep budgie company.

36   Repair service — buttons, electrical appliances, household tasks.

37   Reading — help on a one-to-one basis in schools and libraries, even adult literacy campaign.

38   Odd jobs — wiring.

39   Telephone to housebound or keep in touch.

40   Share — shopping, bulk purchases, home, garden, laundry.

41   Story telling at libraries particularly holiday times.

42   Sunday afternoon drives and teas for others.

43   Talk to clubs and others.

44   Toy repair service.

45   Writing.

46   Wine making.

47   Slimming clubs — give encouragement.

48   Swimming clubs — help children to improve or elderly learners.

49   Retirement courses — organised for and by the retired.

50   Voluntary work.

6 Physical Pursuits

Simply because physical processes have rendered an individual less active than before there is no reason to assume that the capacity to enjoy free time in a structured way is diminished. In fact, with the right attitude many people look forward enthusiastically to the time when they will retire so that they can pursue activities that the need to earn a living prevents.

However, for some elderly people putting the above into practice is often very difficult in a work orientated society like our own, when a change like retirement can mean a drastic alteration in life-style. Coupled with this, the general tendency in our society to value youth and denigrate age means that older people who no longer play an obviously meaningful role in society tend to have a feeling of uselessness and lack a sense of self-worth and dignity. That is why it is important for older people to have a range of interesting and appropriate recreational opportunities available to them, both to fill their long leisure hours and to meet, in a positive way, some of their personal needs. But what are these needs and what contribution does meaningful recreation make to them?

Many studies have demonstrated that physical recreation makes a significant contribution to the physical condition of the aged, particularly in terms of heart function. Exercise helps to relieve tension and to prevent the progressive breakdown of the body systems. Activities that have been found to be beneficial include croquet, billiards and snooker, bowling, hiking, fishing and gardening — all of which provide both pleasure and diversion as well as muscle toning, stretching, healthful relaxation and breathing benefits. In addition to games and leisure activities, a growing number of older persons today are taking part in more vigorous and active sports. In France, for example, older people are encouraged to take part in a wide variety of physical activities including exercise classes, hiking, swimming and cross country skiing.

Obviously, not all elderly people would be capable of such strenuous activity. Such examples, however, demonstrate that we are far too limited in our vision of what older people can accomplish — and of the benefits to be derived from regular, healthy exercise.

Meaningful involvement in social, physical and creative recreational activities tends to improve the state of mind of most aged participants. It takes their minds off the preoccupation with themselves, their illnesses and their problems and provides a sense of accomplishment in performance. In general, it contributes to a positive outlook toward life.

There are many opportunities for older people to participate in activities associated with arts, music, the theatre or literature that awaken or revive creative impulses not felt for many years. Again, these stimulate intellectual functioning and emotional well-being and encourage a sense of vitality and energy.

Recreation can provide an atmosphere conducive to developing friendships and to overcoming isolation and resulting loneliness. Indeed for many elderly persons the social interaction that occurs when a group get together is often more beneficial than the actual activities undertaken.

The selection of suitable activities for the elderly made here is by no means comprehensive and many other possibilities exist. It is more important that people caring for the elderly realise that the experience of becoming participants, and not merely spectators, in whatever activity is pursued, is likely to bring tremendous benefit to older people.

Physical Pursuits

For further ideas contact your

1 Local Recreation and Leisure Department

2 Library

3 Keep Fit Association

4 Sports Centre

5 Bike Hire Centre

6 Swimming Pool

Recommended Reading

1 Leisure and Gardening for the Disabled £2

2 'The New Games Book' – Play Hard Play Fair Nobody Hurt

3 Guide Lines for Jogging   Cunninghame District Council

 # Social Pursuits

The elderly have varied interests and the social pursuits they may care to follow will be governed by this as well as by their mobility, health and financial situation. The list that follows includes many favourite activities for young and old alike, and you may care to add a few of your own ideas at the end: –

1	Art	8	Handicraft
2	Sketching	9	Renovation
3	Bingo	10	Darts
4	Community Singing	11	Drinking
5	Bridge	12	Television
6	Dominoes	13	Church Meetings
7	Hymn Singing	14	Lay Meetings

Social Pursuits

10 Education and the Retired

Education is finding out about ourselves and our world; retirement is an opportunity to spend more time doing so with the enormous benefit of maturity and experience. Below are some suggestions about where older people can find educational opportunities.

The biggest providers of education are the Regional Councils, most of whom now have *Community Education Departments.* Under the banner of Community Education come all sorts of classes and courses which are mainly practical in nature — yoga, dressmaking, lapidary, are examples — but also what is often called 'liberal studies' which includes subjects like politics and social history. Education departments also provide the opportunity to take examination classes in most school subjects if the spur of an external assessment is desired.

Also within the 'public sector' come *community centres* where groups exist to cater for many needs and preferences — pensioners clubs, yoga classes, community associations, photography groups and many others. *F. E. Colleges* cater for examination classes in a wide range of subjects and many are beginning to orientate themselves more and more to less formal provision. The more recent development of the *Community School* in some Regions means that, potentially at least, retired people have the chance, if they wish it, to make wide use of school facilities both during the day and in the evening, and even to join in some classes with school children.

Opportunities do not end outwith the 'public sector' run by the local authorities. *The Workers' Educational Association,* a voluntary organisation devoted to the promotion of adult education, runs a wide variety of courses in and around many of the larger cities. By and large its classes are in liberal adult education — social and general history, literature, politics, current affairs, art and music appreciation etc., — but it also runs courses which cater

Education and the Retired

especially for those who are retired. As a voluntary organisation, the WEA offers the retired person the chance not only to take part in his or her own educational activity but also to participate in the organisation and promotion of adult education for others – perhaps to run Preparation for Retirement courses? The *Extra-Mural Departments* of most Scottish Universities provide similar educational opportunities for the retired as the WEA does. The advantage of the University Extra-Mural Departments is their access to the staff and facilities of the Universities themselves. Some Extra-Mural courses meet the needs of those with more extensive academic interests while others give people the chance to experiment in the laboratory. There are also *University Settlements* which in some cases run a small number of courses but which concentrate on harnessing student voluntary effort to community use. More mature voluntary help is often appreciated. Finally in this category there is the *Open University.* The opportunity at last to be a student at a University is something many retired people take up with enthusiasm and the Open University welcomes them as it does all its students. It is basically first come, first served, as far as entrance is concerned, but once a student has been accepted, the variety of courses offered is very wide and actually graduating is perhaps less important than taking part in what can be an exciting experience.

A number of other educational opportunities exist in most towns and cities. The local *museums* will often have lectures or film shows linked to exhibits, which are themselves an educational resource. Many *libraries* house material about local life and culture and are gateways to the whole world of learning. In the cities the museums and libraries are even more likely to have major exhibitions or local history sections which the retired, like everyone else, can and should use. Many older people will be lucky enough to live near a *Zoo* with its great potential for education and leisure. The *W.R.I.,* the *Townswomen's Guilds,* the *Church Guilds,* the *Rotary* and *Probus* clubs, all provide the opportunity for hearing talks and participating in discussions.

The preceding suggestions are for the elderly who can, as most do, get about. Those caring for an older person who cannot get about are more limited in the things they can suggest. Although we have doubts about them sometimes, television and radio have enormous educational potential. It is important that watching and listening are supplemented by face to face discussion to enable older people to get the stimulation of educational experience through the media. Finally, just because they may seem mundane, books and magazines should not be overlooked as sources of 'education'.

Safety in the Home

Whilst safety is everybody's concern, special attention needs to be paid where elderly people are involved. Prevention is always better than cure.

Many elderly people tend to carry on in the ways they always have, often too proud to accept help, unwilling to sit down to do a job or between jobs, and not realising the potential hazards that arise.

The RoSPA produce a useful checklist covering Fire, Electricity, Gas, House, Furniture, and Fittings. Good lighting is essential particularly at centres of activity or mobility — but beware of trailing flexes. Fire risks can be high but common-sense will reduce this risk. Smoking, drying clothes, deep fat frying are some of the common dangers. Check all heating appliances. Self-help is possible in most instances but some jobs require an expert, such as anything to do with installing heating appliances, wiring and

Safety in the Home

plugs, replacing glass and fixing grab rails. Someone should always have a last look round at night.

Remember the elderly are more likely to have accidents as they become over-tired. Floor coverings may also be 'elderly' and need watching for worn patches and also if they are slippery from polishing or spilt liquids. Grab rails can be provided around the house — alongside steps and in the bathroom. Old slippers, too, may be the cause of accidents.

If any action is becoming difficult you can be sure someone has had a similar problem before and most likely someone has found an answer. Below are some organisations and book titles where useful help and advice may be found.

The Royal Society for the Prevention of Accidents: –

1   Cannon House, The Priory, Queensway, Birmingham B4 6BS (Tel 021 233 2461)

2   41 South West Thistle Street Lane, Edinburgh 2 (Tel 031 226 6856)

Disabled Living Foundation, 346 Kensington High Street, London W14 (Tel 01 602 2491)

Scottish Information Service for the Disabled, 18/19 Claremont Crescent, Edinburgh 7 (Tel 031 556 3882)

Electricity Board, Gas Board, Solid Fuel Advisory Council

Handicapped at Home: Sydney Foott: Design Centre Book £1.85

Action with the Elderly: Kenneth M G Keddie: Pergammon Press.

Safety in the Home

How Safe is the Home?—a check list.

OUTSIDE CONDITIONS

	Good	Fair	Needs Immediate Attention
Easy entrance/exit to/from Street.	☐	☐	☐
Even path or yard.	☐	☐	☐
Handrail by steps.	☐	☐	☐
Well lit.	☐	☐	☐

INSIDE CONDITIONS

	Good	Fair	Needs Immediate Attention
Well lit — stairs.	☐	☐	☐
centres of activities	☐	☐	☐
by bed.	☐	☐	☐
Use of correct light bulbs.	☐	☐	☐
No trailing flexes.	☐	☐	☐
Condition of plugs.	☐	☐	☐
Number/position of plugs.	☐	☐	☐
Meters easily reached.	☐	☐	☐
Electrical aids — Vacuum.	☐	☐	☐
Kettle.	☐	☐	☐
Iron.	☐	☐	☐
Blanket.	☐	☐	☐
Others.	☐	☐	☐
Gas Aids — Date of last check.	☐	☐	☐
Ventilation.	☐	☐	☐
Condition of tubing or taps.	☐	☐	☐
Wearing of sensible clothing.	☐	☐	☐
well fitting shoes.	☐	☐	☐
Clothes drying facilities.	☐	☐	☐

Safety in the Home

INSIDE CONDITIONS	Good	Fair	Needs Immediate Attention
Grab rail by bath.	☐	☐	☐
toilet.	☐	☐	☐
Fire risks from Heaters.	☐	☐	☐
Smoking.	☐	☐	☐
Electric Blanket.	☐	☐	☐
Chimney.	☐	☐	☐
Clothing.	☐	☐	☐
Mirror over fire.	☐	☐	☐
Using candles.	☐	☐	☐
Height of bed.	☐	☐	☐
Bed against inside wall.	☐	☐	☐
Use of high shelving.	☐	☐	☐
Worn carpets/rugs.	☐	☐	☐
Polished/slippery floor surfaces.	☐	☐	☐
Food storage.	☐	☐	☐
cooking arrangements.	☐	☐	☐
tin opener.	☐	☐	☐
Chairs the correct height.	☐	☐	☐
General convenience of home.	☐	☐	☐
Window opening.	☐	☐	☐
Need for special aids.	☐	☐	☐
Telephone.	☐	☐	☐
Emergency call list readily found.	☐	☐	☐

Road Safety for the Senior Citizen

In Great Britain there are ten million people over the age of 60 and seven and half million of 65 years of age. Expectation of life is improving and the 65 year old has now a good chance of reaching 80 years, which means that the number of elderly people is increasing.

Most older people are reasonably healthy and live in their own homes, are perfectly mobile and join in ordinary social life. This involves moving about as pedestrians and coping with modern day traffic, the speed and volume of which has increased considerably over the years. In the interest of self preservation the elderly, as other age groups, have to combine correct behaviour with accurate judgement of vehicle movements. The very old, however, are no longer capable of quick reactions. In addition many drivers appear to have little understanding of the limitations of elderly pedestrians – and have even less patience. Elderly people themselves often have insufficient knowledge of present day traffic conditions and tend to adhere to outdated road behaviour. They also tend to lack awareness of their own physical capabilities and to pay insufficient regard to other road users when they cross the road. It is not surprising therefore that the road casualty rate for the elderly pedestrian is high as statistics prove.

It is important to demonstrate safe conduct in traffic to old people. This can help them to remain healthy and active and to prevent disablement and dependence on others. Injuries are much more serious for the elderly as they often heal slowly and incompletely, perhaps with permanent disablement and loss of mobility. In addition to the provision of physical measures to assist pedestrians, special road safety education and training for the elderly is necessary to keep them informed of changing road conditions and how best to cope with them.

Crossing The Road

The main problem for the elderly is that they tend to

go through the motions of looking but don't actually see vehicles coming. More visual 'scanning' is required – not just looking – particularly of nearside traffic, before crossing the road.

Once elderly persons have started to cross the road they tend to look around for traffic less often than younger people and they are more likely than others to be hit by vehicles on the far side of the road. There is therefore a particular need for the elderly to keep looking and listening all the way across.

Zebra Crossings
These crossings are provided to facilitate the safety of pedestrians while crossing the road. Care should be taken by the pedestrian before stepping onto the crossing. It must be appreciated that drivers require sufficient time and distance to stop.

Pelican Crossings
Pelican Crossings – exercise better control over both pedestrians and drivers and are much more effective than Zebra Crossings.

They are simple to use. Until the button is pressed to actuate the pedestrian phase the signals will remain at green for drivers. The flashing green man indicates that the pedestrian still has precedence over traffic and sufficient time to cross the road. Pedestrians should not *start* to cross when the green man is flashing.

Central Refuges, Reserves and Traffic Islands
These facilities provide a two fold purpose. They separate opposing streams of vehicles and they protect the pedestrian at the half way stage across the road. Pedestrians are advised to pause at the central refuge to make absolutely sure it is safe to cross the remaining half of the road.

General Safety Points to Pass on to the Elderly
Pedestrians should avoid crossing between parked

vehicles. If this is unavoidable, stop at the outside edge of the parked cars and from this position make absolutely certain it is safe to cross. Watch for cars pulling away from the kerb and for reversing vehicles.

Avoid crossing on a bend in the road where there is no clear view of traffic.

Concentrate on traffic conditions when crossing the road — try not to think of other matters.

Take special care when crossing the road at dusk or after dark. Cross under street lights whenever possible. At night wear or carry something white or reflective. Dress up to show up!

Plan the safest routes to your local shop, library, club, relatives etc. Avoid crossing roads unnecessarily.

When walking on roads without pavements, face oncoming traffic, i.e. walk on the right hand side. If in doubt, stop to allow vehicles to pass.

When getting on or off a bus wait until it stops. Never cross the road at a stationary bus, wait until it moves off.

Watch for turning traffic when you have to cross near a junction or side road, particularly traffic coming from behind you.

Try to avoid busy roads during rush hours and in icy or foggy conditions.

Remember, you may not be as quick on your feet as you used to be and your reaction time is probably slower.

If accompanied by young children, it is imperative that you cross roads correctly and use facilities provided. Remember they learn by your example.

All road users, be they pedestrians or drivers should always: —

THINK BEFORE ACTING — THINK AND AVOID ACCIDENT

Keeping Warm

Many elderly people feel the cold more than others; whilst numbers may be at risk because they do not realise how cold they become. Some are reluctant to spend more money on heating; whilst others are at a loss to know what they can do to make themselves more comfortable. Anyone entering an elderly person's living quarters should ask themselves whether it appears adequately heated, and encourage them to take every precaution to keep the cold out and make the best use of the heating arrangements they have. Older people should be encouraged:

1   to keep active throughout the day and thus generate their own heat.
2   to wear several layers of warm, preferably wool, clothing and pay special attention to their hands, feet and even their head. An extra layer should be used when moving from room to room especially at night, when it is also a good idea to warm the bed and nightwear before getting into them, and to keep a warm drink in a flask handy.
3   to make sure they eat well. Nourishing hot food and drinks are important.

Some elderly people are at risk of even dying through not taking elementary precautions and many more may need to be admitted to hospital. Grants may be available for both home improvements and heating. The WRVS may be able to provide additional blankets.

One cosy warm bed-sitting room may be a good arrangement for winter.

Sources of help: —
Scottish Health Education Unit's Resource Pack and/or Booklet — "Keep Warm This Winter".

The Local Doctor.

Citizens' Advice Bureau.

Social Security Office.

The Benefits of Pets

The keeping of pets provides pleasure and companionship to young and old alike. Some important needs in the elderly can be fulfilled when they care for pets and share their lives with them; many frustrations of loneliness and depression can be overcome.

Consideration must obviously be given to the health and mobility of the owner and their domestic situation as well as to the cost of keeping a pet. In communal situations consideration has to be given to other residents and only if those in charge, such as a Warden or Matron, are sympathetic should a larger pet be contemplated. Fish in Aquariums are recognised for their therapeutic qualities.

It is not necessary to take on pets as a permanent responsibility. People at work may be very grateful to an active pensioner who is willing to walk their dog during week-days, schools may welcome someone to look after their animals during holiday periods, and neighbours may be relieved that even a frail elderly person will care for a budgerigar to allow them to get away for a short weekend break.

Many organisations exist to offer help and advice with veterinary surgeons fees, payment of dog licences, cat food, choice of pet, provision of birds and cages, and finding homes for existing pets that are proving too much trouble or while the owner is in hospital. Advice is readily available from the following sources, but look in your local telephone directory to see if there is a local branch.

1   Your local vet.

2   The Scottish Society for the Prevention of Cruelty to Animals: –

19 Melville Street, Edinburgh EH3 7PL (Tel 031 225 6418)

15 Royal Terrace, Glasgow G3 7NY (Tel 041 332 0716)

15 Union Street, Aberdeen (Tel 0224 21236)

The Benefits of Pets

3   The National Canine Defence League, 10 Seymour Street, Portman Square, London W1H 5WB (Tel 01 935 5511)

4   The Companionship Trust, 58 Broadwalk, South Woodford, London E18 (Tel 01 989 4130)

5   Pedigree Petfoods Education Centre, Stanhope House, Stanhope Place, London W2 2HH (Tel 01 723 3444)

6   Dog Aid Society of Scotland Ltd., 165 Gilmore Place, Edinburgh EH3 (Tel 031 229 1846)

7   Cat Protection League, 3 Casselbank Street, Edinburgh 6. (Tel 031 554 5521)

8   Peoples Dispensary for Sick Animals, 55 George IV Bridge, Edinburgh (Tel 031 225 3257)

9   Dog and Cat Home, Seafield Road, Edinburgh 15 (Tel 031 669 5331)

Nutrition

The Need for Food

The elderly need to be able to buy, or to have provided for them enough food of the right kind to keep them in good health. Food not only has nutritional value but also enormous social and psychological value. A high morale is a vital factor in maintaining an interest in life and thus retaining health and independence: — it is therefore important that within limits, the elderly should be able to eat their preferred foods.

In group homes it should be possible for residents to prepare some, or all, of their meals should they wish to do so — it is vital for morale. They should also be encouraged to share meals with their companions.

Thoughtful planning of kitchens can minimize working difficulties. Oven, hob and refrigerator are minimum requirements; freezers can alleviate shopping difficulties and may well be expected by the coming generation of the elderly who have been accustomed to them in middle age.

If they are in reasonably good health, older people normally eat the food to which they have been accustomed all their lives. There is no need to change diet in old age although 1) there may be an exaggeration of faulty food habits developed during earlier years 2) they may require less food if physical activity decreases.

Small frequent meals may be preferred by older people and may be more easily digested. Taste and smell may be affected in old age and seasoning in food become more important in recipes. Books are available which contain appetising recipes and cookery classes may also be organised by local authorities.

If malnutrition is found, the cause may be associated with non-nutritional disease. Causes can be ignorance, social isolation, physical disabilities (arthritis) psychiatric disturbances, poverty, impairment of appetite due to digestive disorders or malabsorption, poor state of dentition, alcohol and drugs.

Drugs Metabolism is impaired in some alcoholics and anaemia can occur; it is also impaired in those taking barbiturates and anticonvulsant drugs and in those receiving cytotoxic agents. Anticonvulsant drugs can also lead to vitamin D deficiency. Certain foods must be avoided if mono-amine oxidose inhibitors are prescribed. Lack of potassium can occur if diuretics are taken over a long period of time. Low vitamin C intake may cause a small impairment in drug metabolism and could account for part of the reduction of drug metabolism ability found in the elderly.

Although the elderly do not require a special diet (they should be encouraged to eat a wide variety of foods) there are some factors concerning diet which are of particular relevance to this age group.

Fluids Adequate hot fluid intake because of increased risk of hypothermia. Older people are more vulnerable to the cold.

Surveys have shown that older people are more likely to suffer from some vitamin deficiencies, especially vitamin C (scurvy) and vitamin D (osteomalacia). For vitamin C, ensure an adequate intake of fruit, fruit drinks and vegetables. For vitamin D, oily fish, margarine and evaporated milk can help increase the dietary intake of the vitamin.

Constipation

Sufficient fibre should be included in the diet as constipation is often a problem with older people — wholemeal bread and cereals, fruit and vegetables help increase the fibre content of the diet. Bran can be taken as a supplement. The coarser variety is more effective and can be sprinkled on cereals or taken in water or fizzy drinks as a medicine if the taste is not well tolerated. It is important to increase the intake of bran gradually if a low fibre intake has been consumed for many years. A feeling of abdominal distension may be experienced for a short time after bran is introduced into the diet.

Iron Lack of iron can cause anaemia so meat, eggs and green vegetables and chocolate can be encouraged in the diet.

Convenience foods and supplements

Older people need to be reassured about the

nutritional standard of these foods if manufactured by reputable firms. Provided the taste is acceptable they can be useful in times of illness or convalescence. The use of a storecupboard, which may be collected over a period of time, is a good idea.

Suggested Basis For An Emergency Storecupboard

MILK — tinned, dried, or long life.

DRINKS — tea, coffee, cocoa, beefy preparations.

SOUP — tins or packets.

MAIN COURSE — tinned fish or meat.

VEGETABLES — dried or tinned, peas, beans.

POTATOES — tinned or instant with Vitamin C added.

PUDDINGS — tins of rice or fruit.

FRUIT JUICE — rosehip syrup, orange, blackcurrant.

BISCUITS — plain, savoury, crispbreads or oatcakes.

BREAKFAST — oats or instant cereal.

COMPLAN — and similar products.

Assessment of the elderly is important in sheltered housing, in order to ensure as much independence as possible. If capabilities are overassessed undernutrition can occur and if capabilities are underassessed this is bad for morale. Aids may be useful for patients with arthritis and other disabilities.

Preparation of food may be more important than the actual food in order to ensure adequate nutrition. e.g. chopping of food, preparation of fruit and rindless bacon.

For patients who have difficulty in swallowing or who have suffered strokes, foods prepared in jelly form can be helpful.

Obesity can be a problem especially if associated with a condition such as arthritis. A very strict reducing diet is usually not recommended but simple advice may be given concerning the reduction of sugar, starches, salt and fried food. If special therapeutic diets are required, medical and dietetic advice should be sought.

References
Medicine in Old age 1974
Articles from the BMJ

Books to read:

1   Catering in Homes for
    the Elderly
    Adviser in Dietetics
    DHSS
    Hannibal House
    Elephant & Castle
    London SE1 6TE.

2   Malnutrition and
    Disease in the Elderly
    Van den Berghs
    Eat Wisely — Stay well

3   Nutrition in the Elderly
    Exton-Smith, A.N.
    Chapter in
    Nutrition in the Clinical
    Management of Disease
(1978) Edited by
John W. T. Dickerson and
H. A. Lee. Edward Arnold.

4   Leaflet
    Eat Well, Keep Well
    Marmite Ltd.,
    Bovril House,
    Southbury Road,
    Enfield,
    Middlesex EN1 1YP.

5   Leaflet
    Eating well in retirement
    The Dairy Produce
    Advisory Service
    Milk Marketing Board,
    Thames Ditton, Surrey.

6   Keeping Fit in Retirement
    National Dairy Council,
    National Dairy Centre,
    John Princes Street,
    London W1M 0AP.

7   Leaflet
    Healthy Eating for the
    Elderly
    British Dietetic
    Association,
    Daimler House,
    Paradise Street,
    Birmingham, B1 2BJ.

8   Easy cooking for one or
    two
    Louise Davies, Penguin

9   Eating for Health
    DHSS   HMSO

10 Kitchen Sense for the
    Disabled or Elderly
    People
    Disabled Living
    Foundation
    Heinemann Health
    Books,
    23 Bedford Square,
    London WCLB 3HT.

11 Cooking for Special
    Diets
    Bee Nilson
    Penguin

Dealing with Crises

Crises can occur at any stage of life, and even if they are of short duration can be a threat to mental health. The strain may alter a person's normal behaviour. A person often seeks out help more willingly during times of mild to moderate stress. But once the crisis reaches a certain threshold, he or she is likely to be overwhelmed by it and become unable to cope, to panic, and to become involved in useless activities. Considerable support may be required to carry a person through this period.

After a certain stage in life, a person's accumulated wisdom and experience may not make up for a gradual slowing down of mental activity. It may be difficult to cope with new situations and there may be an understandable tendency to worry. Memory difficulties may be at the back of many cases — accusations of robbery, incontinence and the feeling of being wronged. Any concern about health matters may not be unreasonable and it is as well to remember that symptoms are as likely to respond to treatment in elderly people as at any other age. Even minor physical illness can become a crisis causing great distress and over-emotional reactions to trivia may heighten other symptoms. The fact that many elderly peoples' capabilities vary from hour to hour or day to day, may lead to misunderstanding by those about them.

In such circumstances a non-verbal communication may often be the most meaningful — a gentle touch on the arm, the holding of the hand or an arm around the shoulders may penetrate a worried mind, especially when the person is also coping with impaired vision, hearing or speech. Often an entreaty to "try harder" or "be sensible" may only trigger off panic and worsening control. Attempted suicide is often the result of being unable to cope with a crisis.

Just sharing a problem with an anxious elderly person can help to remove their feeling of isolation. Offering an ear to listen and hear can be of great therapeutic value.

Dealing with Crises

Providing a place to come to or even just a comforting cup of tea can work wonders. It's important to be understanding and to keep calm so that the situation can be assessed and a decision made as to whether there is need to intervene and if so, which of the many services available may require to be drawn in to help — doctor, home help, social security, police.

News of a partner or themselves going into hospital, may cause disorientation among older people and there may even be problems on their return. A whole family may be involved and even pets.

Death and bereavement are obvious causes of crisis, dealt with elsewhere in this manual. Other situations which might lead to crisis include: separation from some key figure in a person's life, sudden illness, loss of hearing or sight, or speech, a move to a new home, sudden financial crisis resulting from a bill being overlooked, replacement of clothing and furnishings, loss of income, problems with using new equipment. Vandalism and mugging may cause fear; temporary forgetfulness and a charge of shoplifting may involve the police, all of which may bring a feeling of being unable to cope, a feeling of helplessness and futility. A simple problem of something going wrong with a mail order or non-arrival of an expected letter from a loved one can trigger off sleeplessness, strange eating or drinking habits, and other disturbed behaviour patterns.

Confusion may be alleviated by sustained effort at reality orientation.

In all these situations time needs to be allowed for adjustment and allowances made for any abnormal irritability or weeping. Sympathetic understanding is essential. Help in crisis may be obtained from your local:

Citizens Advice Bureau
WRVS
Age Concern Counselling
Service
Social Work Dept.

Occupational Therapists
Physiotherapist
Samaritans
Police

28 Money Matters

A number of comprehensive guides about the financial aspects of retirement are available among them the Age Concern "best seller", "Your Rights" which sells 150,000 of each edition — usually brought out in late November/early December just after the annual uprating of pensions and related benefits. It will only be possible here to give a thumbnail sketch of the main benefits affecting elderly people and to suggest some of those which are under-claimed. Reference will also be made to other sources of information on income in retirement.

Retirement Pension

The retirement pension is paid to women at 60 and men at 65 who have retired from full time work, although it may still be claimed in certain circumstances if a person continues to work part-time after this age. (see earnings rule) The retirement pension is paid to women at 65 and men at 70 whether they are working or not. An extra 25p is paid to people over 80. The full basic rate pension is only paid if national insurance contributions have been paid at the full rate for most of the years since 1948 (or since a person last started contributing at any time between 1936 and 1948). If contributions fall below this level a reduced pension may be paid. Married women who paid the reduced rate of contributions do not receive a full pension of their own though they may get some graduated pension. DHSS leaflet N115 gives more details and should be available at post offices.

Widows and divorcees who reach the age of 60 may be able to claim a single pension on their late husband's contributions when they retire.

Over 80's Pension

People over 80 may have a retirement pension at a reduced rate or none at all. This is because the retirement pension scheme depends on contributions. Some people over this age either made no contributions or insufficient contributions for a full retirement pension because of their age when the scheme was introduced in 1948. An over 80's pension, which does not depend on contributions, is payable to people in these circumstances. The rate is considerably lower than that of the retirement pension described above. Where someone over 80 receives a reduced retirement pension which is less than the current level of the over 80s pension an amount will be paid to make it up to that level. There are conditions relating to the period of residence in the United Kingdom. Claims can be made on forms in Leaflets N1184 or N1177.

Supplementary Pension

The supplementary pension depends on income and on savings but it is an extra amount of money which means that the income of all pensioners who are householders should be just above the level of the retirement pension AFTER rent and rates have been paid in full. It is still sadly the case that some people believe that because there is only a few pence difference between the rate of the supplementary pension and the retirement pension it is not worth claiming. It is important to remember that an allowance is paid for rent and rates in full (usually) on top of the supplementary pension. Also if people claim the supplementary pension it can act as a sort of passport to other help — with heating, special dietary needs, special laundry costs when there is illness, incontinence or disability, glasses, dental treatment and very exceptionally the rental of an essential telephone for a housebound pensioner. Lump sums can also be claimed for essential items and in exceptional circumstances.

Eligibility for supplementary pension and the help for which this acts as a passport depends on savings, but it is possible to have over £1,000 before it affects eligibility for supplementary pension and several hundred pounds in relation to the other extra help. People living with their family, those who are boarders, joint tenants or owner occupiers, people living in residential homes or nursing homes and those in hospital are all treated differently when working out how much supplementary pension they may be eligible for. Details are available in the current edition of "Your Rights". Department of Health and Social Security Leaflet SB1 also describes Supplementary Pensions.

Rent Rebates and Allowances and Rate Rebates

Many pensioners who can't get a supplementary pension can still get help with rent and rates. The amount of rebate or allowance depends on income, who lives in the house, and how much rent and rates are. In the case of a private tenant where rent includes furniture, rebate is not available for that part of the rent, or for services provided by the landlord. Rate rebate does not cover water or sewerage charges. Leaflets are available from local housing departments.

Attendance Allowance

The attendance allowance is for people who are severely disabled, either mentally or physically and have needed the frequent attention of another person by day or by night for at least six months. It is payable at 2 rates, the lower rate if frequent attention or continual supervision is needed either by day or by night, the higher rate if attention or supervision is needed both by day and by night.

The allowance is tax free and payable weekly to the disabled person. Unfortunately many people believe that it is not available to people over retirement age — IT IS. It is *not* available to people in hospital or a local authority home but it is available to tenants of sheltered housing to private patients and to people in private homes. There are conditions about length of residence in the United Kingdom. DHSS Leaflet N1205 which includes claims form DS2 is available from local social security offices. Helpful notes about the claiming of the allowance appear in "Your Rights".

Money Matters

Invalid Care Allowance

The invalid care allowance is payable to men and single women of working age who are unable to work because they have to stay at home to care for a severely disabled relative receiving attendance allowance or constant attendance allowance. They must not be undergoing full time education. It is not means tested and does not depend on national insurance contributions. People receiving the allowance will normally be credited with class 1 national insurance contributions which will preserve their right to contributory benefits such as sickness or unemployment benefit. Details are contained in leaflet NI212.

National Health Service

Most treatment given under the National Health Service is free but there are some things like dentures, dental treatment and spectacles for which people may have to pay part of the cost unless the person is receiving a supplementary pension when these things too are free.

People who are not getting a supplementary pension may still get free treatment if their income is only a few pounds above the supplementary pension level. Department of Health and Social Security Leaflet M.11 gives more details. It is available from local social security offices.

Prescriptions are free for women over 60 and men over 65. There is a box on the back of the prescription form, which should be ticked, and a space for the recipient to sign.

National Health hearing aids are given free on prescription by the consultant. Repairs and batteries are also free. The new National Health Service behind-the-ear aids are becoming much more available now.

Income Tax

Tax rules are difficult for any one to understand. Help is available from the local tax office or bank managers may

Money Matters

be willing to give advice on this and other money matters.

The retirement pension, widow's pension, a firm's pension and any earnings are all taxable and classed as earned income. Only half of a war widow's pension is taxable. Interest from savings or investments (unearned income) is taxable and over a certain income level is taxable at a higher rate. There is a higher personal allowance for people aged over 65 called the age allowance but this is reduced if income is over a certain level. The higher allowance can be claimed for the whole tax year (6th April – 5th April) if a person or their spouse is 65 at any time during the year. More details about taxation and the different levels appear in the current edition of "Your Rights".

Concessions

British Rail now offer a senior citizen rail card to any man or woman aged 65 or more living in the United Kingdom, provided they can give proof of age. Women aged 60-64 can only get one if they show a pension book. Further details are available from the local railway station.

All local authorities in Scotland have concessionary or free fares schemes for pensioners. These differ from region to region – check with the transport department.

The availability of other concessions varies from place to place and may include hairdressing, shoe repairs, launderettes and cleaning, sport, public places such as zoos, museums, stately homes, adult education classes, theatre concerts cinemas, coach tours, etc. Holidays may be available on concessionary rates and one firm, Saga Senior Citizen Holidays Ltd, 119 Sandgate Road, Folkestone, specialises in individual and group holidays for the elderly at home and abroad. The Scottish Tourist Board publish three booklets which may be of interest:

Money Matters

1   "Holidays with Care in Scotland"
     – for individuals who are physically, mentally or
       socially disadvantaged. Sections on useful
       organisations, publications, accommodation and
       amenities in the different regions, transport and
       financial assistance.
2   "Accommodation with facilities for Elderly Visitors
     – lists hotels and guest houses offering reduced
       off-season rates.
3   "Accommodation with facilities for Disabled Visitors"
     – lists hotels and guest houses and some
       specialised accommodation throughout Scotland
       which cater for the disabled.
     All three booklets are available free from the Scottish
Tourist Board, 23 Ravelston Terrace, Edinburgh EH4 3EU.

Other Sources of Information
     Apart from the various Department of Health and
Social Security leaflets and the Age Concern booklet "Your
Rights" referred to, there is always interesting financial
information in the monthly magazine "Choice" which is
published in association with the Pre-Retirement
Association. It can be ordered through all good newsagents
or from CHOICE Subscription Department, Bedford
Chambers, Covent Garden, London WCZE 5HA. The
magazine covers a wide variety of other topics on health,
hobbies, gardening, fashion etc.

     The Pre-Retirement Association also sell a book
"Money and Your Retirement" which deals with income and
expenditure, pensions and state benefits, investment, etc. It
is available from the Pre-Retirement Association, 19 Undine
Street, Tooting, London SW17 8PP.

     "Your Rights" is available for sale from Age Concern
Scotland, 33 Castle Street, Edinburgh EH2 3DN.

     Citizens Advice Bureaux are able to give up to date
free information about most of the matters covered in this
section.

Home Options

One of the most fundamental factors which older people must consider is whether or not their housing is going to be suitable for them once they reach advanced old age or become handicapped by frailty. Then the most important decision they have to make is whether or not to move house.

This is such a personal matter that the decision is for the old person alone, and friends or relatives should confine themselves to pointing out the advantages and disadvantages of both moving and staying put. Too many old people find themselves bulldozed by anxious relatives into a move which seems sensible but which denies them former sources of help and comfort and thus cancels out the intended benefits.

*Sound reasons **for** moving might include:*

1. Existing house too big to heat or clean properly.
   too old to maintain adequately.
   sub standard (outside WC, no bath).
   too isolated.

2. Too many stairs (inside and/or outside).

3. Distance to shops and other services too great.
   too hilly.

4. Too far away from relatives willing and able to help. (This is extremely important. If a move brings the old person close enough to be adequately supervised and cared for then it is particularly desirable).

5. Existing house about to be renovated/modernised by Council necessitating temporary move, permanent move offered.

Home Options

*Sound reasons for **not** moving might include:*

1   Existing house readily adaptable.

2   Neighbours especially helpful.

3   New friends difficult to make late in life.

4   Excellent transport facilities serving present locality.

5   Blind or partially sighted (The trauma of moving and subsequent difficulties encountered in a strange environment far outweigh any advantages expected. Blind people should not be moved from familiar surroundings if at all possible. It is better to move the help to them).

       Among these reasons for and against moving are many variations and permutations so it is always wise to take plenty of time to consider the options and the likely outcome in the short and long term. It is sometimes possible to consult a housing expert and always useful to ask the Family Doctor for advice (or other medical people involved in treatment). A social worker would provide information about services available locally and could find out the situation in other neighbourhoods. Solicitors should be consulted when property transactions are involved.

       Where a move is proposed to a different part of the country, for example to the seaside or rural settlement, make sure the following questions are asked:

1   Are the local services already overstretched by an excess of elderly immigrants?

2   How near is the nearest hospital?

3   How frequent are the buses?

4   Are the shops comprehensive?

5   Is the climate very different from present area?

It is of paramount importance to be realistic. Do not mince words. What is being considered – future frailty, illness, disablement – may never happen, but it does old people no service to pretend it will not. Just as bereavement is inevitable, at least some physical deterioration is also inevitable and both are best faced squarely and accepted.

Some old people quit unsuitable houses to move in with relatives. This can be an admirable solution for some, offering care and company to banish risk and loneliness. However, it produces a situation which is fraught with problems not the least of which is the possibility of clashing personalities. The young may well be very fond of Grandma but take exception to having her grilling them at the breakfast table because they were out late at night.

Remember, too that as people grow older their traits tend to become exaggerated so one who has been domineering, disorganised or difficult will be more so in old age. Multi-generation households can suffer acute distress with no one getting the upper hand, and continuous compromise eroding even the best relationships. The degree of loudness of television or record player can become a Waterloo.

Good intentions are not enough so ask some searching questions and give honest answers before a change is made which may be bitterly regretted.

1   Is the house really big enough to accommodate another generation comfortably (with plenty of privacy for all)?

Home Options

2. Can the old person be allowed a participating role in the running of the household?

3. Have there been major differences in outlook in the past?

4. Is the prospective "carer" any good in times of real illness dealing, for example, with vomiting, dressings, bedpans, soiled beds etc?

5. Is everyone concerned wholeheartedly committed to the idea?

   Unfortunately, small houses suitable for elderly people are in short supply so even if a decision to move has been reached, it may be some years before it can be effected. It is then essential to reappraise the existing house to see how it can be made as suitable as possible for the time being. There is a real danger that old people will allow themselves to drift into a mere existence in a neglected house just because they are expecting to be rehoused soon. "Soon" could be interpreted by them as a month or two but mean a year or two (or more) to the Council whose officer was too soft-hearted (and therefore misguided) to tell them the truth.

   The following checklist will draw attention to the features in any house (existing or prospective) which need to be looked at while suitability is being assessed.

☐ How many rooms? ☐ What size are they?
☐ Are there stairs? ☐ Handrails and bannisters?
☐ Are floors and outside paths even and non-skid?
☐ Is the bathroom too cramped?
☐ Are the fittings easy to operate and firmly fixed to wall?
☐ Is the kitchen fitted with easy clean surfaces?

Home Options

- ☐ Is it well ventilated with cold pantry or room for fridge?
- ☐ Can the windows be opened and cleaned easily?
- ☐ Are the locks secure but manageable?
- ☐ Is the house draught-proofed and insulated?
- ☐ Is the heating adequate and easily controlled?
- ☐ Are the power supplies (electricity and gas) recently tested?
- ☐ Are switches or controls conveniently placed?
- ☐ Is lighting adequate and well placed?
- ☐ Are the roof, guttering and down-pipes in good repair?
- ☐ Are external walls sound and is there a damp course?
- ☐ Is there a garden?   ☐ Is it manageable?
- ☐ Is the house well located for shops, churches etc?
- ☐ Is access free of major roads, hills or hazards?

Finally, a word about house types. Do remember that terraced houses or flats are warmer (or at least easier to heat) than detached cottages or bungalows but where deafness is a problem it may be an advantage to have no-one through the wall who could be disturbed by loud radio, television, conversation or the GPO specially boosted telephone bell.

Modern multi-storey blocks of flats are probably less of a fire hazard than tenement flats because each floor is self-contained and the stair well is generally a fireproof cell where old people could wait safely to be rescued.

Ground floor accommodation may well be less desirable in certain urban areas where vandalism is a problem. Check the situation with neighbours if in doubt.

Most old people will continue to live in what is called mainstream housing, but some will be allocated specially designed Old People's Amenity houses. Local Authorities and a number of Voluntary Housing Associations have built Sheltered Housing which, by and large, is just the same as Old People's Amenity housing but with the added protection

Home Options

of an electronic alarm system and a warden. This comes in all forms – cottages, terraces, flats in courtyard blocks and tower blocks, or other houses, of any age, modernized and converted.

In addition there are a number of organisations such as Abbeyfield or WRVS who provide bedsits, some with their own cooking facilities but shared bathrooms and WC's. Tenants must be capable of self-care.

The "right" house for one old person may be the "wrong" house for another. What matters is that it is a haven and a friend, a home where independence, dignity and individuality can be maintained.

Help Yourself to Security

The investigation into crimes committed against the elderly is a sad business for police officers. The sight of an old person shocked by the discovery that their home has been broken into, their distress at losing treasured possessions or being cheated out of hard earned savings by a glib confidence trickster, or bogus workmen leads to the realisation that our senior citizens must be made more aware of the vulnerable position in which they find themselves in society today.

Old people *are* vulnerable. Brought up in an era when honesty was expected and respected, they are often easy prey to the con-man or thief.

In offering the following suggestions and advice the police aim is to help the elderly to help themselves. But it should be remembered that the crime prevention officer is always available should further help or information be required. He can be contacted through the local police station.

Home Security

Doors

Front doors should be fitted with a good quality mortise lock. The usual latch type lock which is normally found on such doors does not offer sufficient protection. A door chain is a good investment (as is a peep-hole viewer) but never left on all the time. Rear doors should also have a substantial lock supplemented by a tower bolt dropping into a socket in the floor.

Windows

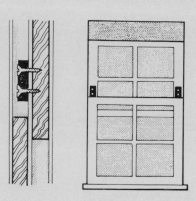

Ground floor windows in particular must have some form of fastening, such as a locking catch. Old fashioned snibs are very easily overcome by the housebreaker and should be replaced. If the windows are required for ventilation only, consider fitting hardwood blocks as shown in this sketch. Upper windows too can present a danger, especially if they are near to drain pipes. The answer here is to have the pipes coated with anti-climb paint.

General

Elderly people going out in the late evening and leaving the house unoccupied, should close the curtains and leave a light on in one of the rooms not the hall light. This will suggest that there is someone at home.

Help Yourself to Security

The elderly should be advised never to leave large sums of money in the house or to carry more than they need when they go out. Knowledge or suspicion of such a practice soon gets to the ears of the thief who then has a target. It is a mistake to think that the home is a secure hiding place – experience shows that housebreakers have a 'nose' for hidden funds. The bank is the only safe place for money in excess of immediate requirements.

Bogus Workmen

Elderly people are the prime target for bogus workmen and confidence tricksters, and the methods used are as varied as the criminals who operate them. The only defence the public has against these people is to *demand* production of some form of authorisation and to examine this carefully in order to establish that the caller is genuine. Public works officials carry identification cards which generally include a photograph of the holder. Elderly people should be advised that if they have any doubt they should refuse admission and notify the police.

They should always be careful about giving information to strangers concerning themselves or their neighbours. There are cases on record of bogus 'market researchers' operating outside supermarkets and post offices, and suggesting that the disclosure of personal details may result in the later delivery of a free sample of some product. The information obtained is then put to use by the criminal. The majority of 'market researchers' are of course genuine, but again they will be in possession of identification which should be produced on request.

The last thing that we would wish to do is to alarm old people unnecessarily but in their own interests they should consider the foregoing advice seriously and if their safety or the safety of their home is at risk, help and advice should be sought through the crime prevention officer.

Legal Aspects

Managing your Affairs

Most elderly people manage their financial and business matters themselves, perhaps with occasional help from their family or friends. If difficulties arise which they can't sort out by themselves (e.g. a dispute with a shop over faulty goods or service, or an Income Tax problem) someone should be found to help. The local Citizens Advice Bureau may be able to solve the problem. If they cannot they will refer the elderly person to someone who can. Several towns in Scotland now have free Legal Advice Centres or Citizens Rights Offices (see the local telephone directory) which may be able to help. Another source of help, particularly if the problem is likely to be large or complex, is lawyers or, for tax questions, accountants.

An elderly person who is unable to cope with financial and business matters, should consider appointing someone else (called an Attorney) to deal with them. Someone trustworthy who is willing to take on the problem should be chosen. For a small fee (£5 — £10) a lawyer will prepare the necessary document called a Power of Attorney (see below for how to find a lawyer and legal aid). Once this has been done the Attorney can deal with bills, pay money into and get money out of bank or building society accounts, deal with any other investments and take over tax affairs. The amount of guidance and instructions he is given should be according to the wishes of the client and the type of work he does. The details can be left to the Attorney.

If an old person becomes completely incapable of managing his or her own affairs then the courts will appoint a person called a *curator bonis*. He may be a member of the family or a lawyer and will take charge of any property and look after other affairs. To prevent fraud he is supervised closely by the courts.

Wills

Everyone should make a will. This sets down how

Legal Aspects

property is to be distributed when a person dies. Money cannot be left to charities, or to people outside your family, or distributed unequally among children without a will. The absence of a will may mean additional worry and expense for the family later.

An elderly person should not make a will without help. The risks of making a mistake are too great, it must be in writing and it must meet certain legal requirements. Will forms are not recommended either, as the instructions tend to be based on English law. Instead advise elderly people to get professional assistance from a lawyer. The small fee (£10) he will charge is well worth it in peace of mind (see below for how to find a lawyer and legal aid). Most lawyers will come out to see people who find it very difficult to get to their office.

The following points will help elderly people wishing to make a will. Before seeing the lawyer they should decide how their property is to be divided, remembering that spouses and children cannot be completely disinherited. Some suitable people (members of the family or friends) should be selected to act as executors. People who are likely to survive the person making the will should be chosen. The lawyer will discuss all these points with the client and also suggest ways of lessening Capital Transfer Tax so that the bulk of the estate is not left to the Government.

Try to avoid changing wills. Not only is it expensive but decisions may get muddled. If people die, grandchildren are born, or divorces occur, then of course it would be perfectly proper to consider a change.

Housing

A common problem for elderly people is that their house may be too big for them to look after or too expensive for them to heat and maintain. What they can do depends on their circumstances. Some possibilities for them to think about are listed on the opposite page:

Legal Aspects

a   They might consider moving into a smaller, easier to run house. Remember they may not be able to drive or get about easily in future. A place near shops, doctors, etc., and accessible by public transport should be chosen. At least one spare room is recommended so that visitors can stay.

b   The house might be suitably divided and part of it let or sold. This is expensive since architects, lawyers, builders and planning permission are required. Some charities operate a scheme whereby in return for a gift of the house, they will flat it and let the owner have one part rent free.

c   It might be possible to move and live with other members of the family. A good idea is to try it for a bit first just to see if it works, before taking any final steps. If the elderly relative can have a separate kitchen and sitting room he or she can be independent or join in as suits everyone best. A drawback is that the older relative will have to move as well if the family moves later.

d   Move into "sheltered" accommodation. This usually consists of small rented units with a warden, nurse etc. who will help when required. Otherwise older people can lead a normal independent life.

e   Move into an old people's home. Private ones are expensive and the fees tend to increase faster than income. In certain cases these increases for those already in a private home may be met from public sources. Local Authority homes accept people on the basis of physical and social need. Drawbacks may be communal living and lack of some independence.

f   Move into specialised residential hotel with all inclusive terms, no restrictions and many amenities.

Moving is a major upheaval and means losing friends in the neighbourhood. It will also be expensive particularly if one house is sold to buy another. An older person going into a smaller place or to a home may have to part with some or most personal belongings — things that have been with them for a long time. They need to be very sure of what they want to do, as it is often impossible to go back. Ask around and get as much advice and help as you can for an old person contemplating a move, especially from others who have had the same problems. If possible arrange for old persons to try places for a time before they make permanent moves out of their own houses.

Special Problems with Rented Accommodation

a) *Local Authorities, SSHA or Local Housing Association property*

There is no security of tenure and tenants can be required to leave at any time. In practice they can stay as long as they like provided they are good tenants. A Notice to Quit is usually given but is not necessary. A spouse is normally allowed to stay on if husband or wife dies but this depends on the policy of the Housing Committee.

b) *Private landlord's property*

Unless an elderly person shares the house with the landlord he or she has full security of tenure, whether the property is let furnished or unfurnished. Even if the house is shared the tenant has some protection. If a Notice to Quit is served and the tenant wishes to stay, or, if a demand for an unreasonably increased rent is made, help should be sought straight away. The Local Rent Officer or Tribunal (address in telephone directory) Citizens Advice Bureau, Citizens

Legal Aspects

Rights Office or a lawyer can all help. Delay in seeking advice may make it too late for them to help. A spouse has the right to stay on in the property after her husband's (or his wife's) death.

Sources of help

a) Solicitors for legal problems. Friends, bank managers or ministers can be asked to recommend solicitors if the old people don't already have their own. Otherwise write or ring the local Legal Aid Committee Secretary (address in telephone directory) or pick a firm from the "yellow pages". In cases of difficulty contact the Law Society of Scotland, 26 Drumsheugh Gardens, Edinburgh (Tel 031 226 7411). Legal Aid may be available if the old person is not well off.

b) Citizens Advice Bureau — Most towns in Central Scotland have an office but there are few in the Highlands and Borders. Addresses in the telephone directories or from Scottish C.A.B., 12 Queen Street, Edinburgh (031 225 5323).

c) Shelter, 6 Castle Street, Edinburgh (031 226 6347) deals with all housing problems.

d) An old person may be lucky and live in a place with a Legal Advice Centre, Citizens Rights Office, or Neighbourhood Law Centre. The addresses will be in the local telephone directory and assistance is free.

e) Local Authority Social Work Departments, or the local church or health visitor may be able to help or at least suggest who to go and see.

First Aid

Important — Read these pages over several times so that you will know what to do if ever the need arises.
Do you know where the nearest telephone is? and the nearest hospital with a Casualty Department?

SERIOUS ACCIDENTS AND INJURIES

A.   IMMEDIATE ACTION in Serious Accidents or Sudden Collapse.

(1)   Make sure no-one else gets hurt.
For example by not attempting to rescue someone from a gas-filled room or burning building: by not touching someone who is still in contact with live electric wiring. On the roads, send someone to warn or stop traffic; switch off ignition and do not allow anyone to smoke.

(2)   Avoid further injury to the casualty.
Don't move the victim unless essential for his or your safety. For example, to avoid risk of building collapsing, to get out of the way of cars, to put out burning clothing by rolling him on the ground (in a rug or coat if possible).

(3)   Turn unconscious (but breathing) casualties onto their fronts with head turned to the side and pulled back. In this position they will not choke and airways are kept clear.

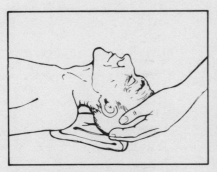 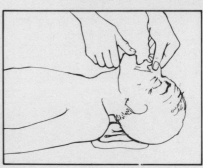

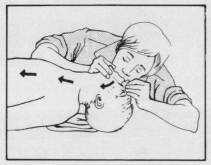 

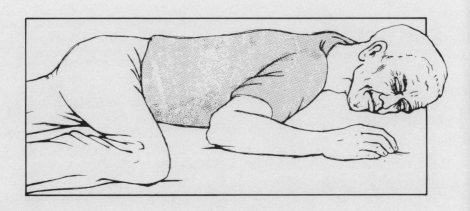

First Aid

(4)   Give the "Kiss of Life" to anyone who is NOT breathing.
This means —

   1.   If possible turn the patient on his back.
   2.   Bend his head well back and support on folded clothing.
   3.   Pull his jaw forward.
   4.   Keep his nostrils closed with your thumb and forefinger.
   5.   Cover his mouth with yours.
   6.   Blow until the chest fills.
   7.   Watch it empty.
   8.   Repeat the last actions (5, 6, 7) each time the chest empties (not more than 20 times a minute).
        Continue until professional help arrives (See over page).

(5)   Stop severe bleeding by pressing.
Don't waste time getting bandages or cloths. Use a handkerchief or a hand. Press the place that is bleeding against the bone beneath or against something hard. If the bleeding does not lessen right away, you are not pressing in the right place, or not hard enough.
If possible, raise the affected part above the level of the breast bone.

(6)   Think
about what still needs to be done, and about how to get help, while you are carrying out these lifesaving measures.

B.   FURTHER ACTION in Serious Accidents and Severe Illness.

First Aid

Patient not Breathing

Continue the "Kiss of Life" until the casualty is breathing regularly or until a doctor tells you to stop. This is the ideal, but you might have to stop because of the need to stop severe bleeding in another person, or because you become too tired to go on. If it is difficult to get air into the person's chest, feel in the mouth to see if there is anything in the way, and check that the head is tilted back and the jaw pulled forward.

The person who has begun to breathe should be turned over on to his front, head to the side and pulled back. HIS BREATHING MAY STOP AGAIN so watch for this and restart the "Kiss of Life" if necessary.

Severe Bleeding

If it can be done without letting the patient bleed again, get dressings or clean cloths. Put a firm pad over the wound, making sure it overlaps all round. Bandage it on firmly. Check that bleeding doesn't start again. If it does, put another pad and bandage on top of the first, or press by hand again. If you see a large piece of glass or metal in the wound, lift it out before pressing, but ONLY IF IT IS LOOSE. Otherwise press around it and around the wound, making sure you do not push it further in.
Unless trained do NOT TRY TO USE A TOURNIQUET.

Large Burns

Once any flames are out, any smouldering clothing can be dowsed with water. Then cover with a dressing or a clean cloth. There is no need to remove clothing over the burn but loosen if possible and remove watches, rings, etc. from burnt part.
Do NOT put on anything else such as butter, burn creams or jellies or antiseptics.

Burns with acids and corrosives need to be washed with plenty of water for several minutes. Watch that the acid is not washed on to some other part of the person; this would cause new burns.

INTERNAL and HEAD INJURIES, Suspected BROKEN BONES, the Person who becomes quickly and obviously ill.
Pain, movement and worry can all make an ill person's condition worse, so aim to keep him as comfortable as possible both in body and in mind. If you think the neck or back may be injured, do not move him if it can be avoided as this could cause paralysis or death. If he must be moved try to do it on some firm support and without bending the back or neck. Use all the help you can get.
Remember that fractures in old people can result from minor falls or injuries.

(1) *Permitted Movement*
Apart from back and neck injuries, unconscious patients should be gently turned into the position described above.
Conscious patients who have not suffered back or neck injuries may be moved slowly and carefully into a position which is more comfortable for them, for example to make breathing easier or less painful.

(2) *Pain*
Pain can only be reduced by preventing movement, yet letting the person relax his muscles. You can help him to do this by carefully padding round the injured part with cushions, folded coats and so on. Do it without moving the injured part if possible.

(3) *Warmth*
Just warm enough to be comfortable, is the rule. This may mean no more than ordinary clothing indoors, or a single blanket outdoors (under as well as over the person). Overwarming draws blood to the skin, away

from important organs which are needing it more. Do not use hot water bottles and never give alcoholic drinks. Both have the same effect.

(4) *Nothing to Eat or Drink*
Any badly injured or ill person may become unconscious. Later, in hospital, he may require an operation. In either case, anything in the stomach could be dangerous as it might be vomited up and then breathed down into the lungs.
If this happens he would choke.

(5) *Reassurance*
It can be very difficult to calm and comfort an ill person. Stay calm and give all the little bits of good news. Don't leave an injured person alone any more than you must. He'll get worried. You may have to answer the same questions every few minutes, if he is very anxious and confused or shocked.

(6) *Getting Help*
If there are other people about, getting help is easy and should be done as soon as you have time to think of it. Usually all that is needed is a 999 call for an ambulance in a serious injury, or call to the doctor (the patient's own if possible) for illnesses. Be sure the person making the call knows (a) who to call and how, (b) what to say is wrong, (c) the exact place or address where help is needed.
A person alone has to decide when he can go for help.

You should never leave someone who has stopped breathing, and very rarely and briefly can you leave someone who is unconscious. Remember injured people can often help themselves (e.g. by holding a wound to stop bleeding) and this will give you time either to help other casualties or to go to get help.

(7)   *Beware of the quick recovery*
People who are knocked out usually get better in a few minutes, assure everyone they are quite all right and want to go back to whatever they were doing. Insist that they should be seen by a doctor within an hour or so for sometimes a concussing injury causes slow bleeding inside the skull. If untreated this can cause death. Anyone who has needed "the kiss of life", even for a minute or two, may become seriously ill after seeming quite well and, therefore, should see a doctor right away.

The person who faints, has a black-out or "nasty turn" for no obvious reason, should consult a doctor at least within a day or two.

Poisoning

There are few poisons which have their own reliable antidote, so treatment is the same for nearly all cases of poisoning: –

(1)   *If unconscious*
Position as for unconsciousness from any cause – turn casualties onto their fronts, with head turned to the side and pulled back.

(2)   *If conscious*
Since the patient may become unconscious, ask at once what has been taken, and how much. If possible, find out name and address, who his doctor is, and where his family and friends are.

(3)   *All cases*
Get medical help as quickly as possible either by 'phoning a doctor or dialling 999. The police come to all 999 calls whichever service is requested. Keep all bottles, containers, tablets, vomit and so on. They may help the doctor to choose the best treatment quickly.

(4)   *Specific Poisons*

Aspirin Overdose — the person may seem well and active for some hours, then suddenly become very ill and die. Do not wait. Get a doctor quickly.

Paracetamol ('Panadol') Overdose — death may result from damage to the liver some days after poisoning unless treatment is started quickly.

Corrosives — if something has been taken which burns the mouth and throat give mouthfulls of water or milk UNLESS THE PATIENT IS ALREADY UNCONSCIOUS.

Dizziness and Giddiness

A feeling of lightheadedness may be caused by: —
- hunger
- too heavy a meal
- alcohol (some people feel dizzy on very little)
- standing up too suddenly, especially in old people.

Sitting or lying down until the feeling passes off is all that is necessary. You should consult your doctor if you have a sensation of "everything going round" and a feeling of general unsteadiness which is more than just a temporary "swimmy" feeling.

Fainting

Fainting is a temporary loss of consciousness which can be caused by such things as: —
- fright or excitement
- sudden shock (bad news or witnessing an accident)
- a hot bath
- standing upright suddenly and too quickly especially after being ill
- loss of blood.

The immediate action necessary is to restore the flow of blood to the head. This is easily done by laying the person down on his front with his head turned to one side and pulled back (see p. 49). Loosen the clothing around the neck and waist.

If consciousness is not regained within a minute or two, CALL THE DOCTOR AT ONCE.

If conscious leave the patient lying down until fully recovered.

If there is any tendency to repeated attacks of dizziness or fainting the doctor should be consulted.

Stroke

A stroke starts with a collapse or seizure, either sudden or coming on within an hour or two. There may be loss of speech and inability to move the limbs on one side. There may be unconsciousness and an alteration in the shape of the face.

SEND FOR THE DOCTOR
While awaiting the doctor: –
- the patient should be laid quietly in bed and kept warm
- dentures should be removed
- brandy and other alcohol should not be given
- nothing by mouth should be given to an unconscious person
- if there is vomiting turn him on his side with the head lowered so that there is no danger of vomit being drawn into the lungs.

Pains in the Chest and Heart Attacks

Pains in the chest that are not obviously due to a muscular strain or that don't clear up should be discussed with the doctor.

If a person gets a sudden gripping pain across the front of the chest get him into a position which is comfortable and which allows him to breathe easily, then call the doctor.

The pain may also be felt in the arms or neck and the patient may be pale and sweating may feel faint or become unconscious. This may be a sudden heart attack.

There is another form of heart attack in which the patient becomes breathless and wheezes for no obvious reason (see below). Make him comfortable and call the doctor.

Having a heart attack is a warning that all is not well. It does not usually mean that you are "done for". Far from it.

Pain on Walking (Angina)

Some people find that if they walk fast they get a severe gripping pain in the chest, the neck and jaws, the arms, or in more than one of these places. If they stop the pain goes away, but if they try to go on the pain gets so bad that they have to stop. This is not a heart attack but it does need the doctor's advice.

Tightness in the Chest

Tightness in the chest or wheezing or difficulty in breathing should always be discussed with your doctor.

Coughing

Any persistent cough or one accompanied with breathing difficulty requires the doctor's advice.

Coughing up blood should always be reported to the doctor EVEN THOUGH IT OCCURS ONLY ONCE.

Breathlessness

We all get breathless if we run too fast, carry too heavy loads, and so on. This is normal. The effort needed to make us breathless depends upon age and fitness. If a person becomes breathless more easily than others of the same build and way of life, he should consult his doctor.

CALL YOUR DOCTOR, even during the night: —
- if there is much wheezing and breathlessness at rest if there is difficulty in getting the air in and out of the chest.

Palpitations

This is the feeling of the heart thumping in the chest. The thumping may be fast or irregular. It does not mean that the heart is diseased. It can happen to many people, including healthy young athletes.

Attacks are often started by alcohol, smoking, coffee or tea, tiredness or worry (including worry about the heart). Often they are noticed in bed at night.

Only if attacks are very frequent need the doctor be consulted.

Very fast heart beats which do not slow down in ten minutes or so can reduce the efficiency of the heart and the DOCTOR SHOULD BE CALLED at once unless he has given other instructions after a previous attack.

MINOR INJURIES
Cuts and Grazes

Small wounds should be cleaned carefully and gently with soap and water, or with a mild antiseptic in the strength recommended by the makers. Thereafter they can be covered with an adhesive dressing or bandage. Wounds heal better if the air can get to them through the covering.

Medical attention is needed if: –
- the wound is very deep
- the wound gapes open (perhaps only when a nearby joint is bent)
- it is impossible to get all the dirt out
- there is loss of feeling in nearby skin, or the part "won't work" properly
- the wound has been made by an animal, as it is then more likely to have the germs of tetanus ("lockjaw") in it.

Splinters

Splinters of wood, glass or metal must be removed, or the wound is likely to become infected. Try to lift them out with small forceps (eyebrow tweezers are good). If this is not possible, they can often be eased out with a needle which has been boiled for three minutes to kill germs. The point can be used to push aside the skin over the splinter, and then to lever it out.

Small thorns and the like can be left, as they will work themselves out in a few days.

Get medical help for very large or very deep splinters.

Burns

Small burns and scalds should be cooled in cold water for five minutes, either in a bowl or under the tap. This helps the pain and stops further damage. Thereafter the burn should be covered with a sterile, or at least clean dressing. Burns with a blistered area more than, say, two inches across should be seen by the doctor or nurse at the next consulting hour, or as soon as an appointment can be arranged.

Burns larger in size than the patient's hand URGENTLY need medical treatment.

Insect Bites and Stings

For most people bites and stings are no more than a nuisance. If the insect has left its sting, lift it out, (taking care if the poison bag is still there not to squeeze more poison in). Then dab with something cooling like Calamine Lotion. Traditionally, diluted ammonia has been used for bee stings, and vinegar for wasps, but there is little advantage in this.

Some people are allergic to certain insects, and become rapidly and dangerously ill. They need medical help urgently. So too does anyone who has been stung by a bee or wasp inside the mouth or throat, because swelling may interfere with breathing.

Things in the Eyes

Small bits of dust, sand and so on which get into the

eye, and can be easily seen on the white of the eye, or inside the eyelids, can be wiped off with a clean handkerchief or a paper tissue. Wipe gently towards the nose.

Never attempt to take out anything which is firmly stuck, or which lies on the central clear part of the eye near the pupil.

Chemicals and Household Liquids in the Eye

Wash out at once by holding the eyelids open with the fingers, and pouring water in, or putting the face in a basin of water. Continue for five minutes. Then go to the doctor or hospital Casualty Department.

Bleeding Nose

Except when the nose is broken, bleeding nearly always comes from the lower fleshy part. Like anywhere else, pressure stops the bleeding, but here press by holding the nose firmly between finger and thumb, below (NOT over) the nose bones. Get the person to do this while he sits still, leaning forward over a bowl or basin and breathing through his mouth. He must hold it for at least five minutes by the clock, and then let go slowly. Blood clots can be pulled away before he starts, but the nose must not be touched or blown afterwards, even if there is still a little dripping. If this method does not work even after a second attempt, get medical help. Do not try to pack the nostrils with tissues or cotton wool.

First Aid Box and Medicine Cabinet

Most households keep a few dressings and bandages, and one or two home remedies. Here is a suggested list of contents so that you will have what is required when it is needed.

First Aid

First Aid Box: –

   for Serious injuries
   2 slings (triangular
   bandages)

   2 large wound dressings
   2 medium wound dressings

}   these are packets
   containing
   dressing pad and
   bandage all in one

   for Other Injuries
   Bottle of antiseptic
   5 individually wrapped gauze swabs (preferably non-
   stick)
   3 conforming bandages 2″ or 3″
   Box of adhesive dressings (assorted sizes)
   Round ended scissors 5″
   Tweezers

Medicine Cabinet
   Painkillers like soluble aspirin or paracetamol
   Indigestion tablets
   Calamine Lotion

   Do not clutter up the cabinet with medicines
used regularly. These should be kept somewhere safe
and convenient for the user. Do not keep left-over
medicines "just in case they'll be useful." Many of
them lose their effect or become dangerous. Put them
down the lavatory or return them to the chemist for
disposal.

   Your first aid box and medicine cabinet must
be handy when needed, but safe out of the way of
children.

First Aid Note:
   You cannot learn the proper care of illness or
injury from books alone, and there is only room for a

First Aid

few simple principles in this one. Why not join a First Aid Class? Find out about them from your local St. Andrews Ambulance Association or Red Cross Society. The numbers and addresses are in the telephone book.

 # Danger Signs

The elderly are more liable to fall ill than the rest of the population and illnesses can be multiple and complex.

In addition the presentation of illness by old people is frequently much less dramatic and florid than illness presented by younger people. Old people tend to be fatalistic about their disabilities and often they will not seek advice for conditions which would take younger people rapidly to a doctor. This is because they are apt to feel, "I'm too old, doctor", or "There's nothing to be done at my age anyway", or "You must have more worthwhile patients than an old person like me".

General indicators that things are not quite as they ought to be are:
(1) "Failure to thrive" – general, non-specific deterioration – a phase borrowed from paediatrics.
(2) Recurrent falls.
(3) Onset of mental changes – usually confusion.

Specific conditions which are liable to be missed by people caring for the elderly are:
(1) **Bladder disturbance** – The old person goes more often to the toilet and is up several times at night. Old ladies may begin to wet themselves on coughing or sneezing and try to "cover up" or pretend that all is well.

Danger Signs

(2) **Bowel disturbance** —Usually the problem is constipation which may be either chronic and longstanding or may be provoked by an acute illness with fever and loss of appetite and being bedridden for a spell. In the case of the former, expert medical and nursing help is required and will need to be continued indefinitely. Where the constipation has occurred recently it is necessary to be sure that there is no growth or other serious condition. Constipation may paradoxically present as "diarrhoea", because the bowel has become so overloaded that it cannot be emptied normally and only small ineffectual motions are passed. Danger signs are loss of appetite, the old person spending longer in toilet, and, more frequently, evidence of faecal soiling.

(3) **Failing vision** – Old people are inclined to assume that the spectacles supplied at age 60 will "see them out", not realising that stronger lenses may be necessary, or that cataracts may develop (which nowadays can be easily treated). Obvious difficulties in reading newsprint, in seeing T.V. should be treated seriously and advice sought.

(4) **Hearing problems** – Even more than with vision, old people are apt to be slow and reticent in seeking help despite the fact that much can be done to help with hearing loss. Sometimes all that is necessary is to have the ears syringed to remove plugs of wax.

(5) **Problems with walking** – The most common problem is with painful feet due to corns, callouses, bunions and other conditions which can be remedied. Old people often allow themselves to become quite lame without seeking help and any old person who is walking badly or who persistently flops about in old slippers should be suspected of needing chiropody. The problem may only be thick long toenails which they cannot cut themselves.

Other locomotion problems arise from painful stiff joints usually at the knees or hips. These cause considerable disability and limitation of life style. The joints may look swollen, hot and red, or may be less obviously abnormal. Sudden onset means that something has gone seriously wrong and it may be gout, acute sprain or other treatable state. Immediate help is necessary since every day an old person spends "off the feet" makes it increasingly likely that he or she will not regain the former level of mobility.

(6) **Falls** – Anyone can fall but the old are more liable to do so. About half of all falls are due to tripping and stumbling, due to poor lighting, irregular floors, etc. The other half result from loss of accuracy of balance associated with poor vision, degeneration of the nervous system and the results of stroke. An old person who has fallen once is at risk of further falls and the next one may lead to serious fracture and the patient may never walk again. Recurrent falls may be the first sign of serious general illness of almost any type.

Falls are serious.

(7) **Mental illness** – This presents by far the most difficult set of problems for those involved with the old. There are two common conditions – dementia and depression.

Dementia is a progressive loss of mental capacity due to disease which eventually leads to severe impairment as a result of which the sufferer may be almost helpless. Early detection is important because, although there is no treatment known at present, the patient needs careful management and his or her supporters need help and encouragement.

In both movements the direction of movement of the trunk should be oblique to upright on standing, and from standing to oblique after grasp is established, then upright to sitting.

Similar basic principles obtain when using toilets or bed.

WHEELCHAIR USERS
Wheelchair to Bed
Chair is slightly angled to bed. Transfer can be straight forward or sideways or if back can be removed, backward transfer — ensure brakes on.
Lift legs on bed.
Arm of chair removed.
Hand on bed — hand on chair.

Beds
The bed should be low enough to sit on and high enough to facilitate standing. The provision of a rope ladder, a monkey pole or a vertical fixture will aid this transfer.

Wheelchair to Toilet
A sideway or a backward transfer can be performed with the help of aids or adaptations. A raised toilet seat will facilitate transfer and will help where limitation of movement of the hip joints makes sitting lower painful and difficult.

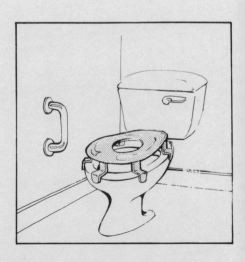

Chair and Wheelchair to Bath

The illustrations demonstrate the types of aids and adaptations which will facilitate transfer. For transfer in the bath added security may be provided from a higher to a lower seat with back supports.

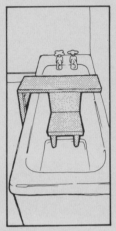

Use of a Sliding Board

If the arm movements and power of the muscles is deficient or if the distance between the transfer points is too great, a sliding board can facilitate transfer to bath, bed etc.

Walking Aids

It is important that walking aids are chosen with care. They must be the correct type and the correct length and dimension.

Walking Sticks

Measure for walking sticks from the crease of the wrist to a point about 6″ in line with the heel of the footwear. The elbow should be bent to about 15°. If the strength and movement of the grip is deficient, a padded grip can be added to facilitate control.

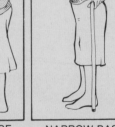

WIDE BASE   NARROW BASE

Moving Around

Crutches
The grip should be at a
similar level to that of
sticks while the length
measurement should be
taken from just below the
armpits to about 6″ in line
from heel. There must be no
pressure on the armpit. All
weight is taken on the
hands.

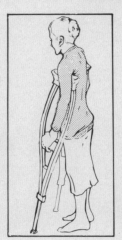

Tripods and Quadrupeds
Measured as for sticks,
these are usually provided
for adjustable height.

Walking Frames
The height should allow for
more bend of the elbow to
allow for lifting and
reaching forward.

There are many varieties of the above aids — care
should be taken in the suitable choice while maintenance —
ensuring the security of screws, rubber tips etc., — should
be undertaken before and during use.

Care of the Feet
In addition to other deficiencies which may be aided
e.g. glasses, hearing aids, aids to daily living, the care of the
feet is of the utmost importance in preserving mobility, while
the provision of suitable footwear enhances getting around
safely, comfortably and independently.

Aids and Adaptations
Aids and adaptations to assist in daily living and
getting around are available but ideally anyone requiring
these should be assessed and only equipment which is

absolutely essential provided, modification of everyday
items already in use may suffice.

Maintenance of Mobility

Circulation and muscle control will be maintained by
being as mobile as possible. Suggestions for activity
schemes for the elderly are outlined in the references below,
while more comprehensive advice on transfer and lifting
techniques are contained in the publications indicated.
These contain valuable information to enhance moving
around comfortably, safely and with dignity.

References

HANDLING THE HANDICAPPED
CHARTERED SOCIETY OF PHYSIOTHERAPY
Woodhead Faulkner Ltd. £2.50

RETURN TO MOBILITY
THE CHEST, HEART AND STROKE ASSOCIATION
Margaret Hawker MCSP £1.50

RETURN TO INDEPENDENCE
THE CHEST, HEART AND STROKE ASSOCIATION
Truda Wareham MCSP £1

LET'S GET MOVING: AGE CONCERN
Eira Davies £1

HELP YOURSELF
P Jay, E Walker, A Ellison: Butterworth 75p

PHYSIOTHERAPY HELPS NURSING
NURSING TIMES
MacMillans Journals Ltd.

SELF AIDS: THISTLE FOUNDATION
W M Davis GROT, MHOT.

CARING FOR ELDERLY PEOPLE
Susan Hooker MCSP: Routledge & Kegan Paul £3.95

Moving Around

In both movements the direction of movement of the trunk should be oblique to upright on standing, and from standing to oblique after grasp is established, then upright to sitting.

Similar basic principles obtain when using toilets or bed.

WHEELCHAIR USERS
Wheelchair to Bed

Chair is slightly angled to bed. Transfer can be straight forward or sideways or if back can be removed, backward transfer — ensure brakes on.
Lift legs on bed.
Arm of chair removed.
Hand on bed — hand on chair.

Beds

The bed should be low enough to sit on and high enough to facilitate standing. The provision of a rope ladder, a monkey pole or a vertical fixture will aid this transfer.

Wheelchair to Toilet

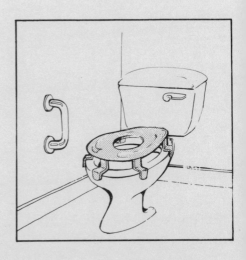

A sideway or a backward transfer can be performed with the help of aids or adaptations. A raised toilet seat will facilitate transfer and will help where limitation of movement of the hip joints makes sitting lower painful and difficult.

Chair and Wheelchair to Bath

The illustrations demonstrate the types of aids and adaptations which will facilitate transfer. For transfer in the bath added security may be provided from a higher to a lower seat with back supports.

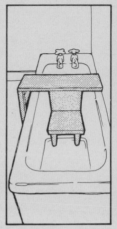 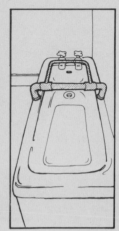

Use of a Sliding Board

If the arm movements and power of the muscles is deficient or if the distance between the transfer points is too great, a sliding board can facilitate transfer to bath, bed etc.

Walking Aids

It is important that walking aids are chosen with care. They must be the correct type and the correct length and dimension.

Walking Sticks

Measure for walking sticks from the crease of the wrist to a point about 6″ in line with the heel of the footwear. The elbow should be bent to about 15°. If the strength and movement of the grip is deficient, a padded grip can be added to facilitate control.

WIDE BASE NARROW BASE

Crutches

The grip should be at a similar level to that of sticks while the length measurement should be taken from just below the armpits to about 6″ in line from heel. There must be no pressure on the armpit. All weight is taken on the hands.

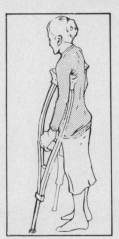

Tripods and Quadrupeds

Measured as for sticks, these are usually provided for adjustable height.

Walking Frames

The height should allow for more bend of the elbow to allow for lifting and reaching forward.

There are many varieties of the above aids – care should be taken in the suitable choice while maintenance – ensuring the security of screws, rubber tips etc., – should be undertaken before and during use.

Care of the Feet

In addition to other deficiencies which may be aided e.g. glasses, hearing aids, aids to daily living, the care of the feet is of the utmost importance in preserving mobility, while the provision of suitable footwear enhances getting around safely, comfortably and independently.

Aids and Adaptations

Aids and adaptations to assist in daily living and getting around are available but ideally anyone requiring these should be assessed and only equipment which is absolutely essential provided, modification of everyday items already in use may suffice.

Maintenance of Mobility

Circulation and muscle control will be maintained by being as mobile as possible. Suggestions for activity schemes for the elderly are outlined in the references below, while more comprehensive advice on transfer and lifting techniques are contained in the publications indicated. These contain valuable information to enhance moving around comfortably, safely and with dignity.

References

HANDLING THE HANDICAPPED
CHARTERED SOCIETY OF PHYSIOTHERAPY
Woodhead Faulkner Ltd. £2.50

RETURN TO MOBILITY
THE CHEST, HEART AND STROKE ASSOCIATION
Margaret Hawker MCSP £1.50

RETURN TO INDEPENDENCE
THE CHEST, HEART AND STROKE ASSOCIATION
Truda Wareham MCSP £1

LET'S GET MOVING: AGE CONCERN
Eira Davies £1

HELP YOURSELF
P Jay, E Walker, A Ellison: Butterworth 75p

PHYSIOTHERAPY HELPS NURSING
NURSING TIMES
MacMillans Journals Ltd.

SELF AIDS: THISTLE FOUNDATION
W M Davis GROT, MHOT.

CARING FOR ELDERLY PEOPLE
Susan Hooker MCSP: Routledge & Kegan Paul £3.95

Moving Around

HELP FOR HANDICAPPED PEOPLE IN SCOTLAND
DHSS and Department of Employment

CHRONICALLY SICK AND DISABLED PERSONS
ACT 1970
HMSO

The Scottish Information Services for the Disabled, 18/19 Claremont Crescent, Edinburgh will provide further information regarding equipment, services and facilities available.

They also have a mobile exhibition which tours Scotland and which contains many examples of aids, adaptations equipment through M.A.C., mobile aids centre.

The British Red Cross Society publish information on aids and usually have a lending scheme.

Statutory authorities, Health Boards, Social Work Departments and Housing Departments and voluntary organisations along with the General Practioner and his team will be able to provide further information and support.

Rehabilitation Engineering Movements Advisory Panels, at Thames House, North Millbank, London, a project of the British Council for Rehabilitation of the Disabled offer engineering help and advice on mobility.

Further information is available in the publication "Equipment for the Disabled" intended for professionals produced by the Nuffield Orthopaedic Centre.

Communication

The care of the elderly may be complicated by disorders of communication. This not only affects daily management but also the happiness and well being of the older person through frustration as a result of inability to express emotions and opinions as well as basic needs. For this reason such difficulties require sympathetic understanding.

There are no disorders peculiar to the geriatric population but the following are some of the more common causes of communication difficulties. Very often a combination of disorders is present.

1 *Stroke or other diseases* affecting the brain and nerve supply will result in disorders of speech and language if the part of the brain that deals with these functions is affected. It may be that
   a) the person does not fully understand what is said to him (receptive dysphasia)
   b) he cannot organise words and sentences to express himself (expressive dysphasia)
   c) speech is slurred with poor control of loudness pitch and breath (dysarthria)

Ability to read and write may or may not be affected.

2 *Laryngectomy* this is a condition in which the larynx (voicebox) has been removed because of cancer. It may be that the person has learned how to make a new voice — Oesphageal voice or he may be using a vibrator — a small machine that makes a "voice" noise for him.

3 *Hearing loss* if mild may only affect comprehension in noisy surroundings if profound it may mean the person is almost totally 'cut off'. It is tempting to treat hearing loss as part of growing old — it may, in fact, simply be wax or some other remediable condition and for this reason should be examined by a doctor. It may also be that hearing losses go unnoticed and the person is described as being "difficult" or "confused"

when they give inappropriate answers to questions etc. Some degree of hearing loss may further complicate the other disorders.

There are certain basic principles to be borne in mind when caring for someone who has impaired communication.

Firstly, understanding is vital — loss of the ability to communicate is traumatic and the person may feel everyone is going to think he has "gone daft". Therefore reassurance that one understands what has happened can immediately ease the situation.

The person must be given time to communicate in quiet surroundings to allow him to use his remaining skills of communication most effectively.

If comprehension loss is involved it is important to speak clearly and simply to the person — that means using simple sentence construction, this need not be childish. Do not speak about the person in front of him — he will understand some of what is said and may pick up the wrong meaning. Give him as many extra clues as possible to recognise. Use gestures, written word (provided this skill is not also lost) and pictures.

If expressive ability is impaired make sure you allow time for communication and, again, make available aids such as paper and pencil or pictures.

In cases of hearing loss, the minimum of background noise is essential. Allow the person to see your face when you talk. The light source should be behind the elderly person.

Sometimes ill fitting dentures may be adding to a communication problem — if this seems to be the case the person should see their dentist.

If reading ability is impaired vision should be checked.

Communication

Obviously this is a superficial account of communication 'disorders and their management'. If the person has been in hospital they are likely to have been assessed by a Speech Therapist, however, if they have been cared for at home, the General Practitioner should be able to refer him to a Speech Therapist, who would then give more specific advice.

 # Aids to Daily Living

With the progression from middle age to old age, tasks and activities performed in younger years may become more and more difficult. These difficulties, although they may not stop older people going out, are irritations that make life less comfortable. As in so many cases, the minor problems may manifest themselves in other, more major, unnecessary symptoms of ill health or depression. If the quality of life can be improved, then growing older does not need to be a frustrating progression to becoming dependent on outside help.

Community Occupational Therapists are employed by the Social Work Department to help the elderly and physically handicapped to be as independent as possible within their own setting, be it home, sheltered housing or residential accommodation. The Community Occupational Therapist can supply aids to daily living, suggest adaptations to property and other general help with any difficulties.

The range of aids to daily living cover all aspects of self care and although some of them are listed here, it is advisable to contact the Occupational Therapist who will be aware of what to look for and where to find the best aid to suit your specific needs.

Aids to Daily Living

The Community Occupational Therapist works from a Social Work Department Area Team and any member of the public can request a visit for themselves or for a friend.

What areas become difficult for elderly people to cope with?

Household chores: It may be that bending down, or stretching to dust is difficult, for a variety of reasons e.g. painful arthritic joints or dizziness.
Available aids include:

> long handled dust pans
> long handled dusting sticks
> helping hands to pick up that magazine on the floor.

If rising from an easy chair is a difficult task for an older person, an orthopaedic chair may help.

Kitchen: Making a meal can mean a great effort. Trying to turn on taps, open jars, open tins, carry the tea pot to the cup even lifting the cup by the handle can be difficult for the elderly. Bear in mind the O.T. who can supply:

> Tap turners
> Jar openers
> one handed or easier tin opener
> tea pot stands
> special cups
> plates with raised lips

Eating: Holding a knife and fork may pose problems as some old people just cannot manage to grip the cutlery tight enough.

Perhaps more suitable cutlery can be provided, or handles built up to make the grip more comfortable and secure.

Dressing: Some elderly people find socks and stockings difficult to get on or they may trip round the house all day with shoe laces undone. Perhaps a stocking aid and elastic shoe laces could overcome this. And what about little shirt buttons? Perhaps a button hook or pieces of velcro could solve this difficulty.

Toilet: An old person may experience difficulty in rising from the toilet unaided.
> By raising the toilet seat a couple of inches in a soft
> or firm material, providing a grab rail,
> or putting arms round the toilet,

any worries about getting up safely can be overcome.

Bath: Many elderly people are unable to get in or out of the bath. By attaching a rail to the taps, or a grab rail on the wall, along with a small raised seat and non slip mat many people can have a bath without fear of being unable to get out.

One of the biggest problems faced by people caring for the elderly may be helping to lift them in and out of the bed and the bath and on and off the toilet. By using a free standing mobile hoist — a smaller neater version of the type seen in hospital, any weight can be lifted and without strain. The O.T. can provide this type of aid and advise on problems relating to the lifting of old people. All the aids mentioned are simply set up by the O.T. and involve no fuss or mess and can be removed if unsuitable.

If however, the main difficulty for an elderly person is getting in and out of the house, the following adaptations can be provided:
> hand rails inside and outside,
> adapt steps to suit a Zimmer walking aid,
> create a ramp to suit a wheelchair.

Some elderly people are at risk if left unaided, and in some cases a channel of communication in emergencies is vital in such cases. The Social Work Department may approve the installation of a telephone.

Aids to Daily Living

For elderly people who have a good neighbour or family close by, it is possible to install a simple alarm system from one house to another. On turning a switch a light or bell comes on to indicate that help is needed.

Some aids are supplied by the National Health Service:

i.e. bed aids: Monkey poles, bed cages ⎫
    commodes   ⎬ District Nurse
    leg rests   ⎭
    walking aids – Zimmer, sticks ⎱ Community
    Wheelchairs for frequent use   ⎰ Physiotherapist

Application for these aids must be made through a General Practitioner. The Red Cross provide wheelchairs on a temporary basis for holidays or special outings.

If expert advice is required, the O.T. might recommend organisations which deal with specific problems. There are other areas, however, where the O.T. will pass you on to other organisations where you can get the benefit of expert advice.

Help for Blind or Partially Sighted Elderly People:

There are various aids to help the blind or partially sighted elderly to manage everyday activities and leisure pursuits. These include:

Special tactile watches and clocks make it possible to "feel" the time.

A small hook over the lip of a cup which buzzes when a tea cup is full.

Dominoes with large raised spots help those whose sight is no longer what it used to be.

For registered blind or partially sighted older people who cannot read the large print books available at all Libraries, even when used with a magnifier, "talking books" with a wide range of tapes are available.

It is also possible to supply a blind person with a radio.

The Radio Times is printed in braille.
Information from the Royal National Institute for Blind.

Help for the elderly, deaf and hard of hearing: Devices available include:

    door signals
    light and vibrator alarm clocks
    adaptors to amplify the sound on a telephone

    A useful aid to have installed for listening to the T.V. or radio, whether in the common room of a Home, or Sheltered Housing, or in the family living room, is the Inductive loop. The deaf person is not attached to T.V. by any wire. A suitable hearing aid picks up the signals in the form of magnetic waves.

The R.N.I.D. publish a synopsis of T.V. programmes.

Further information is available from: Royal National Institute to the Deaf.

Both the Electricity Board and Gas Board provide aids for some of their appliances:
Examples include
    Loop handles on electrical plugs for people with arthritis and
    special knobs for cooker or fire switches.
Pamphlets are available from showrooms.

    All these aids are of great help, whether installed in the home, in sheltered housing, or in residential accommodation.

    These aids are available free of charge and it should be emphasised that they can be installed with no fuss or disruption to the elderly person.

    The following organisations can advise anyone who wishes to pursue any of the ideas mentioned:

Aids to Daily Living

Community Occupational Therapist
Based in Social Work Department throughout the Country.

Red Cross

Local Offices from
Head Office or
telephone directory

Alexandra House
204 Bath Street
Glasgow, G2 4HL
041 332 9591

Royal National Institute for Blind

244 Great Portland Street
London W1W 6AA
01 388 1266

Society for Welfare and Teaching of the Blind

4 Coates Crescent
Edinburgh EH3 7AP
031 225 6081

Royal National Institute for Deaf

9a Clairmont Gardens
Glasgow G3 7LW
041 332 0343

Edinburgh and East of Scotland Society for Deaf

49 Albany Street
Edinburgh EH1 3QY
031 557 0419

The local branches of these societies are listed in the
telephone directory.

MAC's TRACKS — a mobile display of aids
Scottish Council on Disability
19 Claremont Crescent
EH4 4QD.

Bereavement

Bereavement should be regarded more as a social than a medical occurrence and the tendency for it to be made into a disease is one which society should examine with great care. After a social blow such as death or an accident to a near relative it is not necessary to go into a state of suspended animation and to be "under the doctor". The appropriate company after a death is the company of one's relatives and friends. The presence of the doctor with his bottle of sedative tablets is of very doubtful value as sedation merely postpones the necessary grieving which will have to be enacted before recovery from loss is likely to occur.

There are two major contributions which other people can make during the bereaved phase. One is simply to be present with the bereaved person preferably during the daily activities of life and such a presence is valuable for the intermittent discussion of feelings, regrets and future fears. The other point in the presence of relatives and friends is to help with the immediate practical questions of registration, funeral, and financial matters concerned with house, bills, etc., which may well have been the function of the deceased. Where a bereavement is imminent it is well to identify coping relatives who should know in advance that such practical considerations may fall to them for action. Major decisions such as giving up one's house, going to stay permanently with relatives, or giving away sums of money or of property should not be taken during bereavement. To stay with a relative or friend for two or three weeks is desirable but a return to one's house at an early point is quite essential in order that the necessity to think and act should not be endlessly deferred. During the period of stay the receiving household should not be paralysed and sit looking at the bereaved person but should continue with its usual activities and the bereaved person should be involved in these rather than regarded as a patient to be looked after.

The bereaved may react in a large variety of ways and

Bereavement

sometimes will move from one variety of reaction to another. Such reactions, as total inertia, "collapse", anger, bitterness, despair, recrimination against all who are trying to help, and feelings of desolation and loneliness are very common. Time heals most of these reactions but visitors for quite some time after a bereavement, perhaps even up to a year, may have to be very patient and continue visiting no matter what their inward feelings may be. During this phase it should be noted that hallucinations involving the deceased are common and bereaved persons quite often think they hear the voice or even see the form of the deceased moving about the house. These reactions also fade with time.

Bereavement is a variety of loss and the elderly who are bereaved may have already experienced other losses, e.g. family, health, ambitions, good times, and sometimes other varieties of bereavement such as loss of a limb. The bereaved elderly frequently react less emotively to loss because the inevitable is one which they have been living with for many years, both as regards their own mortality and morbidity and that of the deceased relative.

After return home the difficulties of facing the world alone may seem insuperable and the bereaved person may have to start for the first time to think of a considerable number of difficult matters e.g. finance, domestic functions which they have never had to consider before. This may increase their feeling of helplessness and bitterness so that some practical home help may be appropriate for a short period at this time. Where there is no near relative and if the bereaved person is significantly isolated then the Cruse organisation will be found most helpful both for comfort and practical advice. The general principle underlying help during the time of bereavement should however be those of robust acceptance of what must be accepted rather than sentimentalising in the past and certainly rather than reducing the patient to an inert cypher for whom everything must be done.

Bereavement

The death of one spouse however may show for the first time the weakness of the survivor. When the support of the deceased has been removed it may be seen for the first time that the surviving relative is significantly mentally and/or physically impaired. In the months that follow bereavement a true depressive illness may make it's appearance with loss of appetite, and weight, abnormal sleep patterns and attempted suicide. The appearance of such reactions must be looked for by relatives and social and medical helpers of all kinds. Dissolution of the extended family society as well as the removal of highly concentrated housing areas have combined with the decline in religion to increase the isolation of the bereaved. The older the person the more likely it is that their lives have withdrawn from the institutions and organisations of society (anomie).

It is not to be expected that the reaction of the bereaved will be one of unalloyed grief and despair. Where the bereaved has been giving much support and where the final illness has been distressing the over-ruling sensation may be one of relief both on one's own behalf and also on behalf of the deceased that suffering has not continued. It should be realised that death occurring in an elderly household is not necessarily the most catastrophic and important loss which the bereaved person may have experienced. Death in age is not premature and is frequently not an unwelcome guest. The acceptance of death in age is one of the major characteristics of late life although the bereaved may seem a pathetic relict to relatives and friends.

Where no close relatives are available the Cruse organisation or the undertaker frequently are able to advise on matters far outside the realm of mere disposal of the dead.

The following references may be of some value.

Bereavement by C M Parks. Penguin/Pelican 1972.
Death and the Family by L. Pincus. Faber 1976.

Index

Index

1

S
Safety 12,14-15,39-42
Security 39
Sheltered Housing 38,45,84
Shopping 5,14,65
Social Activities 8,65
Social Security 27
Solicitors 35,43-47
Speech 26,78
Sport 6-8
Stress 26, 36
Stairs/steps 14,71
Strokes 56,78
Suicide 26,88
Supplementary
   Benefits 29-31
Swellings 64-68

T
Telephones 3,15,29,38
Television 12,36,38,84
Tension 6
Toilet 62,63,67,73,82
Traffic 16-18
Transport 32,45

U
Universities 11
Unconciousness 48

V
Ventilation 38
Vision 26,35,60,63,69,79,83
Voluntary Work 5,8

W
Walking Aids 69,74,75,82,83
Warmth 19,69
Wheelchairs 73,82,83
Wills 43
Windows 37,40
Workers' Education
   Association 10
W.R.V.S. 27,39

Z
Zoo 11

92

Acknowledgements

Contributions have been welcomed from members of the following Departments, Organisations and Professions: –

Department of Geriatric Medicine, Edinburgh.
Scottish Sports Council.
Workers' Educational Association.
Lambs House, Leith.
Lothian and Borders Police.
Queen Margaret College.
Age Concern (Scotland).
Scottish Law Commission.
Physiotherapy.
Occupational Therapy.
Speech Therapy.
Social Work Services Department.
Scottish Health Education Unit.